Dedicated to Jenna

This is a book about looking for a clue...

To find missing things from my house.

One minute there...

Then gone!

As fast as a mouse!

One minute we can find everything...

The next minute we're scratching our heads!

Mom is asking "Where's my red scarf?"

Dad is asking, "Anyone see my ties?"

My sister is crying because she lost her first prize!

And I've lost my gaming device!

So I decide to become a detective

Just like
Sherlock Holmes.

Because he knows what to do...

Jump Jump Jump
And look for a Clue!

I need all my senses

To figure things out.

SMELL

TASTE

TOUCH

SIGHT

HEARING

And my super sniffer puppy will help us to...

Jump Jump Jump and Look For A Clue!

Clues can be anywhere I'm not looking

They can be difficult or easy to find..

That's why you always need to keep an open mind.

You never know what you're going to find!

It's like the clue wants to find you!

Arthur sniffs the air and leads the way...

He IS THE CLUE!
And now it's time to...

Jump Jump Jump
Because we love
LOOKING AND FINDING
CLUES!

I

LOOKING FOR

Clues!

Other books in the
Jump Series:
Jump Like a Caribou!
Jump Like a Kangaroo!
Jump at the Zoo!
Jump and Say P.U.!
Jump and Say Boo!
Jump and Say Valentine's Day Is
For Kids Too!
Jump and Say Who-Who!
Jump For Everything Blue!
Other Children's Books:
The Three Boulders
Billy Shakespeare
Billie Shakespeare

www.ingramcontent.com/pod-product-compliance
Lightning Source LLC
Chambersburg PA
CBHW051602120626
46551CB00013B/1640